PET HERMIT CRAB

by Robin Nelson

first step nonfiction

Lerner Publications Company · Minneapolis

A hermit crab is an **animal.**

Hermit crabs make
good **pets.**

Pet hermit crabs live in a
tank called an **aquarium.**

Hermit crabs need
a clean aquarium.

Hermit crabs do not like
to be too cold.

Hermit crabs do not like
to be too hot.

Hermit crabs need food.

Hermit crabs eat
almost anything.

Hermit crabs need
water to drink.

Hermit crabs need to keep
their bodies wet.

Hermit crabs need **shells** to **protect** themselves.

Hermit crabs need new shells
when they grow bigger.

Hermit crabs like to climb.

Hermit crabs like to be
with other hermit crabs.

We like to watch
our hermit crabs.

We like taking care
of hermit crabs.

Parts of a Hermit Crab

The tail and lower legs of a hermit crab are hidden inside its shell. The lower legs hold on to the shell. They have a large pincher claw to defend themselves and climb. The small pincher claw is used for eating and climbing. The jointed legs are used for climbing and walking. Hermit crabs have eyes that can move in any direction. Hermit crabs have two short and two long antennae. These are used to smell, hear, and feel.

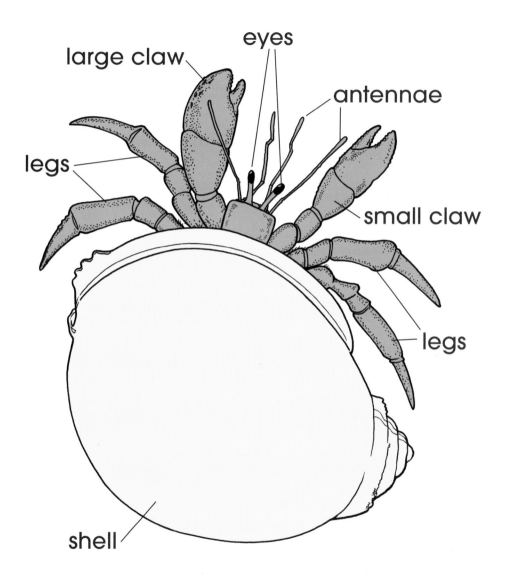

large claw

eyes

antennae

legs

small claw

legs

shell

Fun Hermit Crab Facts

 If a hermit crab loses a leg, an eye, or an antenna, it will grow a new one.

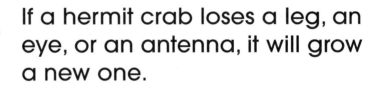 Hermit crabs need to keep their bodies wet because they have gills. Their gills are near their legs. They use their gills to breathe.

A hermit crab is about the size of a golf ball.

 A hermit crab carries its shell on its back. Its shell is like a house that protects the hermit crab.

 Hermit crabs live for two or three years.

Glossary

 animal – anything alive that is not a plant

 aquarium – a glass box

 pets – animals that live with people

 protect – to keep safe

 shell – a hard covering on the outside of something

Index

aquarium – 4

bodies – 11, 18–19

climb – 14

food – 8, 9

shells – 12, 13

water – 10, 11

Lerner Publications Company
A division of Lerner Publishing Group
241 First Avenue North
Minneapolis, MN 55401 USA

Website address: www.lernerbooks.com

Library of Congress Cataloging-in-Publication Data

Nelson, Robin, 1971–
        Pet hermit crab / by Robin Nelson.
            p.   cm. — (First step nonfiction)
        Includes index.
        Summary: A simple introduction to hermit crabs and how to care for them as pets.
        ISBN: 0–8225–1270–X (lib. bdg. : alk. paper)
        1. Hermit crabs as pets—Juvenile literature. [1. Hermit crabs as pets. 2. Pets.]
    I. Title. II. Series.
    SF459.H47 N46 2003
    639'.67—dc21   2001005913

Manufactured in the United States of America
1 2 3 4 5 6 – AM – 08 07 06 05 04 03